BE
YOUR
BEST
YOU

First published in Great Britain in 2021
by The Watts Publishing Group
10 9 8 7 6 5 4 3 2 1
All rights reserved

Editor: Nicola Edwards
Cover design: Jason Anscomb, Rawshock Design
Inside design: Matthew Lilly
Cover and inside illustrations
by Roberta Terracchio
Consultant: Clare Arnold, psychotherapist with 25 years'
experience working with CAMHS, the NHS's Child and
Adolescent Mental Health Services

978 1 4451 7407 5 (hardback)
and 978 1 4451 7408 2 (paperback)
Printed in China

FSC
www.fsc.org
MIX
Paper from
responsible sources

WHAT IS A TRUSTED ADULT?

Throughout the book we suggest you speak to a trusted adult. This is a person who makes you feel safe and that you can trust. It could be a parent or carer or another family member, such as an aunt or uncle or grandparent. It could be a teacher or someone you know well, such as a family friend or a friend's parent or carer. Or it could be someone at the end of a helpline (see pages 172–174).

BE YOUR BEST YOU

Honor Head

W
FRANKLIN WATTS
LONDON • SYDNEY

CONTENTS

BE YOUR BEST YOU

Being your best you doesn't mean being rich or famous or having the latest trainers or the most likes on social media. It means being strong physically and mentally, being happy and kind. It's about being successful in what you do, whether it is knitting a scarf, finishing your science homework or playing in a football match. It also means being interested in the world around you.

The best you is the person you want to be, not what anyone else wants you to be. Yes, you should listen to advice from your family, teachers and supportive friends, but this is your life and you have to live it in a way that makes you feel happy and proud of yourself.

Trying to be your best you can sometimes seem hard, especially when you feel tired, lonely or scared, or friends are putting pressure on you to do something you don't feel is right. Plus, there might be times when you are worried about a problem, and unsure how to deal with it. This book is here to help. It is divided into four chapters that look at all aspects of life.

YOUR BRAIN AND BODY will help you to understand how your physical and mental health are closely linked, and give you tips on how to improve both.

YOUR EMOTIONS looks at your feelings and moods and how they help to shape your behaviour.

STRESS AND ANXIETY affects everyone at some time. This chapter will help you to recognise the signs of feeling stressed and anxious and give you tips on how to cope and feel better.

SOCIAL MEDIA is brilliant but it can also cause problems. This chapter explains how you can use social media in a fun and safe way and stay in control.

TRY THIS!
Look out for these boxes throughout the book. They will give hints and tips on quick ways to improve your mental health that you can do every day or whenever you need to.

YOUR BRAIN AND BODY

THIS CHAPTER EXPLORES HOW YOUR BRAIN WORKS WITH YOUR BODY AND HOW MINDFULNESS, POSITIVE THINKING AND PLENTY OF SLEEP CAN HELP YOU FEEL LIKE YOU CAN TACKLE ANYTHING. YOU WILL ALSO FIND OUT HOW YOU CAN DEVELOP A GREAT BODY IMAGE AND GOOD SELF-ESTEEM.

DREAM TEAM!

Your brain and body work as a team. What you do with your body affects your mood, while your thoughts and feelings affect how you feel physically.

Blink, breathe, chew!

Can you think of things your body does without you having to think about it? For example:

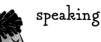
speaking

blinking

chewing and swallowing food

shivering

sweating

It does all these things with the help of your brain. Your brain is working 24 hours a day, every day you're alive — even while you're asleep. But your brain doesn't run the show alone; it is helped by your nervous system. The nervous system is a complicated bundle of nerves inside your spine. These nerves connect to every part of your body, from your eyes to your toes. Your body and brain use the nervous system to send messages back and forth to each other all the time.

Red alert

Your nervous system is always on red alert. If something dangerous is about to happen, such as if a ball is speeding towards you or you're about to touch a hot pan, your brain and nervous system react immediately and make you dodge the ball or pull your hand back from the hot pan.

11

Neuron power

We're born with a brain and nervous system, so why don't we automatically know how to read or walk or ride a bike? When you're born your brain is equipped with millions and millions of neurons (nerve cells). Each neuron has tiny branches coming from it that can connect to other neurons ... a bit like lots of people reaching out and holding hands to form a line. The neurons start to connect when you start to learn things, when you learn to walk, talk, read, play football, dance. Once you start to learn, the neurons make connections so that the activity becomes easier and easier until you do it automatically.

HELLO, BRAIN!

So now we know how important the brain is, let's have a quick look at how it works.

The cerebrum

The biggest part of the brain is called the cerebrum and it's the part that controls your voluntary muscles. So when you play football, dance or just get out of a chair, this part of your brain is working to get the muscles you need to move. The cerebrum also helps you to think. It helps you do your homework and figure out how to win a video game. That's not all. It also controls your memory and reasoning, such as deciding whether something is a good or a bad thing to do.

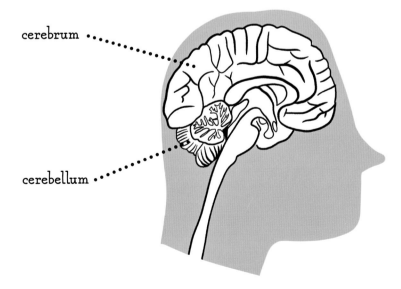

cerebrum

cerebellum

The cerebellum

Whether you're skateboarding,
surfing or just walking in a straight line, you
need your cerebellum to keep your balance and
coordination. This is the bit of the brain that controls how
your muscles work together.

The brain stem

Your brain stem is connected to your spine and keeps
you alive. It is in charge of your involuntary muscles: all
those muscles inside you that you never think about, such
as your heart and muscles around your lungs that keep
you breathing.

The pituitary gland

This part of the brain is especially important to preteens. The pituitary gland is only the size of a pea but it has a massive effect on your body when you reach puberty. During puberty the pituitary gland releases hormones into your body that start your physical body changes as you grow and develop into an adult (see page 16).

Emotions centre

It's not just your actions that your brain controls. It also controls the way you feel, your moods and emotions. Whenever you feel sad, happy, disappointed, angry, scared or any other emotion, these feelings are coming from a part of your brain called the amygdala (say: uh-mig-dah-lah).

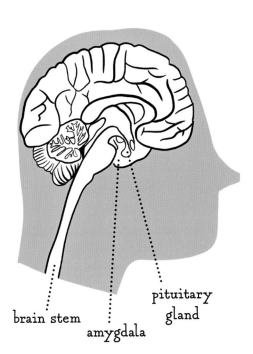

brain stem

amygdala

pituitary gland

Brain care

So now you know how important your brain is, you can see how it's important to look after it as much as it is to look after your body. As we'll see in this book, what you do to your body affects your brain, and how you use your brain affects your body. Your physical health and mental health are closely linked.

HORMONE HAVOC!

Puberty creates hormone changes in the brain. These not only affect your body but also the way you think and feel.

Physical changes

During puberty your body changes from a child's body into an adult's. You might have growth spurts, where parts of your body like your arms and legs suddenly grow much faster. Boys start to develop muscles, their chest and shoulders become broader and they start to get more body hair, especially on their chest.

Girls start to develop rounder hips, their breasts start to grow and some girls may grow more body hair. Both boys and girls might start to sweat and smell more. All these physical changes are perfectly normal.

16

Mental changes

All the hormones that flood your body during puberty also affect your brain and your moods and emotions. This can lead to huge mood swings — one minute you can feel on top of the world, the next you might hate everybody and think everybody hates you!

The hormones will affect each person differently. You might feel suddenly irritable and grumpy, the smallest thing might make you feel like shouting and slamming doors: you might think no one understands you, that everyone's against you and the world has suddenly become a strange and frustrating place.

Emotion commotion

Some young people becoming teenagers might also feel sad and anxious about what is happening to them or in the world around them. These mixed emotions can make you feel even more worried and maybe a bit frightened about what is happening to you. What you are feeling is all perfectly natural. However, if you do feel overwhelmed by sadness, anger, anxiety or by your feelings and if your moods are affecting your schoolwork and ability to enjoy life, you may need to speak to a trusted adult and see a doctor to make sure everything is okay. Don't be ashamed or embarrassed to ask for help; puberty is a challenging time and everyone reacts to it in their own way.

18

TRY THIS!

If you feel as if your head is about to explode or is filled with bad thoughts, try to calm your body and mind by doing a simple breathing exercise. Find a quiet place. Breathe in through your nose for a count of four. Hold it for a couple of seconds, breathe out through your mouth for a count of five. Repeat until you feel calmer.

EAT WELL

What you eat not only keeps your body and brain healthy, it can affect your moods and how you cope with everything.

Getting it right

Eating the right amount of food and the right type of food keeps your body in good condition and your brain healthy. It also helps you to cope with mood swings and negative emotions when they do happen. A healthy diet is one that includes a lot of fruit and vegetables, some protein such as meat, fish, lentils and beans or vegetarian protein such as tofu, and carbohydrates such as brown pasta and rice. Try and keep sweet things such as ice cream and cakes for special treats.

How does what I eat affect my brain?

We've seen how your brain has a lot of work to do and to do it properly it needs the right fuel. Nutrients, such as vitamins and minerals, from food give you energy to keep yourself going and to grow and develop properly. These nutrients also keep all the nerves and neurons in top condition so you can concentrate on schoolwork and learning. A healthy diet helps to keep the parts of your brain that control your emotions and moods in good working order, too.

A diet overloaded with fast food or ready-made meals, which contain lots of sugar and chemical additives, can make you feel sluggish, anxious and grumpy. A healthy diet makes you feel alert and happy and helps you to cope with everyday stresses much better.

Well watered

Your body needs water to stay healthy and so does your brain. Water also keeps your brain sharp and stops you feeling tired, fuzzy and muddled. If we get dehydrated it makes us feel irritable and grumpy. Keeping well hydrated improves concentration, helps us to stabilise our moods and feelings, eliminates toxins from the blood, keeps brain cells healthy, helps us sleep better and improves blood flow and oxygen to the brain. Wow!

How much water you need to drink depends on your age, weight and how active you are. Drink a glass of water with meals and when you feel thirsty. If you're being active or it's warm, make sure you have water with you. As well as drinking water, you get water from fruit and vegetables so have plenty of these in your diet. Sugary drinks don't count!

TRY THIS!

If you have trouble remembering to drink water, get in the routine of having a glass or mug of water when you get up in the morning and one before you go to bed.

ISSUES WITH EATING

There are many reasons why some people develop eating disorders.

What are eating disorders?

Two eating disorders you may have heard of are anorexia nervosa, when someone believes they are overweight so stops eating or eats very little, and bulimia nervosa. Bulimia is when a person stuffs themselves with food and then purges themselves — makes themselves sick or takes laxatives to go to the loo a lot. Food binging or compulsive eating is similar, but the person may not purge themselves. All eating disorders seriously damage a person's health and in some cases can even be fatal.

Why do they happen?

Eating disorders can happen when a person has experienced an emotional trauma, such as a family breaking up, being put into foster care or someone dying.

Developing an eating disorder is a way for that person to feel they are in control of their lives by controlling the food they eat, when the world around them has become out of control and a frightening place.

22

Every day we are bombarded with images of slim, glamorous people who seem to have the perfect lifestyle. This can make some people think that if they were slimmer they would be happier, have more friends and a better life. They start to obsess about their weight and what they eat, and this develops into an eating disorder. Some children have parents who are weight-obsessed and this passes on food anxieties to the children.

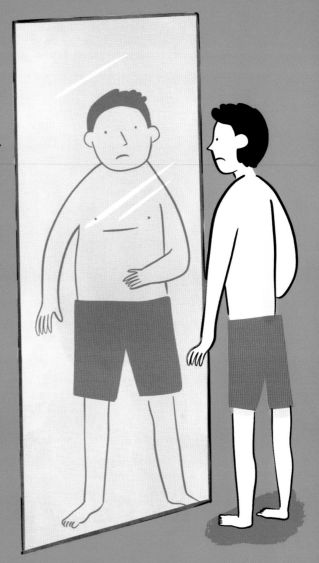

Getting help

Whatever the reason for an eating disorder, if you think you might have one it is essential to get professional help. There is no need to feel scared or ashamed to talk to someone. Speak to a trusted adult or phone a helpline (see pages 172–174) and make sure you get some medical advice. If you think a friend has an eating disorder and they won't do anything, speak to a trusted adult on behalf of the friend or suggest that the friend speaks to an adult they trust. The sooner your friend gets help the sooner they'll get better.

When my parents started to argue I would grab handfuls of food and sit in my room and eat and eat until I felt sick while I heard them shouting at each other. Eating and then being sick became a way to cope with unhappy things, and I found I was binge eating if I got poor test results, had a silly argument with my friends or any small thing really. Eventually my parents split up and I rang a helpline about my eating. I talked to Mum and we went to see the doctor. I'm not binge eating so much now and I feel much better mentally and physically.

Stuart, 15

SELF-ESTEEM

What we think of ourselves is a good indication of our mental health.

All my fault!

Self-esteem is what we think of ourselves. Self-esteem is about liking and trusting ourselves, and being proud of who we are. Most of us, for all sorts of reasons, can be very hard on ourselves. We think we're not good-looking enough. We're no good at art or useless at sport. Our schoolwork is not good enough and we are always embarrassing ourselves. If we don't get picked for a school team, lose a game or a friend dumps us, it's our fault. But let's face it, not everything can be one person's fault!

Positive bounce back

People with good self-esteem will be positive thinkers, ready to give anything a try. People with low self-esteem think they will fail before they've even started and imagine no one will like them or want to be their friend so why try. It's not easy, but you can change how you feel by how you think. If you ever think "this is too hard", or "I can't do this", stamp out the negative thoughts and think, "I can do this", "I'll give it a try". Even if you don't get it quite right, you'll feel better about yourself because you tried. Remember we talked about neuron power in your brain (pages 11-12)? Well, the more you say "I can" and "I'll try", the easier it will become and before you know it you'll be trying things without even having to think about it.

26

Love yourself

You are special and unique. There really is no one else like you. Think about what makes you special — it might be your great sense of humour, kindness, willingness to help or being a good listener.

If there is something about how you look that's troubling you, think about whether you can change it in some way. If you can't, you can decide to accept it and focus on what you like about the way you look, such as your lovely nails, great hair or nice eyes. Spend time with friends and family who love you and make you feel special and safe.

27

TRY THIS!

It may seem a bit strange at first, but give yourself three compliments a day that have nothing to do with how you look. It could be that you made a great sandwich for lunch, finished a test at school, made your friend laugh or offered to help in the kitchen. Soon your brain will become tuned in to more positive thoughts.

BODY IMAGE

A positive body image is linked to your self-esteem and how you feel about yourself.

Media gloss

On television, in magazines and online we see celebrities and models, both male and female, who look perfect. But life just isn't like that. These images and online videos have been prepared, filtered, glossed and tweaked to look the way they do. This doesn't stop many of us comparing ourselves to the images we see all around us and thinking we should be prettier, have bigger muscles, longer legs and flatter stomachs. We begin to hate the way we look and this becomes a negative body image. A negative body image is not just about how you look, it can affect your whole life.

You can begin to think that if only you were thinner, or taller or had smoother skin you'd be happier, have more friends and a lot more fun.

Social media

Nasty comments about how you look on social media can also affect your body image. If the comments are deliberate this is a form of bullying. If this happens to you tell a trusted adult or phone a helpline (see pages 172–174). There is no need to be ashamed; it is the bully who needs to be ashamed. Talking will help you to realise that what is being said is untrue and stop you feeling isolated. Block anyone who is being abusive – this takes away their power and helps you regain control.

How do you know if you've got a body image problem?

Do you:

Refuse food or go hungry because you think you need to lose weight?

Always comment on people's weight or their shape?

Think about how you look all the time?

If you said yes to any of these, it could be that you need to have think about how you see yourself. For a start, learn to be proud of your body – after all, it can do amazing things. Be proud that you are strong and healthy. If you do think you might be overweight, speak to a trusted adult and see a doctor to check out that everything is okay. If you want to be fitter, set yourself some goals and plan a routine. Setting yourself goals and achieving them will make you feel better mentally, and you'll be physically fitter too.

You are not perfect

No one is perfect. You need to accept that you may not be perfect but that you have lots of very special qualities that have nothing to do with the way you look. When you start to worry about how you look, think about something you do well or really enjoy, such as being with your best friend, looking after your pet, trampolining or football.

> *I was worried about being unfit as I don't like the sport we have to do at school. I enjoy watching kung-fu movies and my mum suggested that I try out some different martial arts to see if I'd like doing them as much as watching them. Now I go to judo every week. It's made me much fitter and I feel a lot healthier too. I love it!*
>
> **Alex, 13**

SWEET DREAMS!

Getting enough sleep and good quality sleep is important for us mentally and physically.

Why is sleep so important?

Young people need long periods of sleep each night to help their body and brain to grow and develop. While your body is resting, your brain can focus on filing away what has happened during the day. During sleep the neurons in your brain are strengthened and renewed, helping to improve concentration and memory. Scientists have proved that sleep helps us to learn better and remember more. Experts believe a young person aged between 9 and 11 needs about 9.5 hours of sleep a night.

Tired and moody

Not getting enough sleep can also affect your moods. If you haven't slept well you can feel tired, grumpy and irritable the next day. It is harder to feel positive and upbeat when you are tired, and this could lead to negative thinking and dark moods. You are also more likely to make mistakes if you are tired, which can make you angry or affect your self-esteem. A good night's sleep means you wake up feeling refreshed, energised, positive and looking forward to a new day.

32

Sleep zone

Try these tips to make your room a better place for a good night's sleep.

• Turn off your computer and phone an hour before bed as the blue light from digital screens can overstimulate areas of the brain making it more difficult to sleep. Instead, choose a book by your favourite author and have a read before you sleep.

• Make sure you are comfortable — not too hot or too cold.

• Try to go to bed at the same time every night so that your brain and body get into a routine.

• Be active and try not to nap during the day. But don't do anything too energetic just before bedtime!

33

TRY THIS!

If you can't sleep because you're worrying about something, see if these tips help:

● *Take your worry and lock it in a worry box (in your head). Say you'll take it out and look at it again in the morning.*

● *Write your worry down on paper and then tear it into little pieces or crumple it into a ball and throw it away.*

● *Decide you will talk to someone about your worries in the morning. This will make you feel better as you now have a plan of action to deal with the problem. This puts you back in control. Sweet dreams!*

ALWAYS TIRED

> Sometimes stress and worry can make us oversleep and still feel tired.

Yawn!

For some people, stress and anxiety can make them sleep too much. This is the brain's way of coping — by switching off. If you find you are sleeping a lot but still feel tired, grumpy and have a foggy brain, are you worrying about something? Some worries can niggle away in our mind without us really being aware of them, and the brain tries to cope by shutting down. This is obviously not a good thing when you have school and a social life. Take some time to sit by yourself somewhere quiet and calm, breathe deeply and see if anything comes to mind that could be worrying you.

Body clock

You may have heard of your body clock — this is the natural rhythm of your body. It is called your circadian rhythm and is how your body deals with physical and mental processes over a 24-hour period. Your body clock affects your temperature, appetite and sleep cycles. The hormone changes that happen during puberty will affect your body clock. You may find that as you go through puberty you want to go to bed later and sleep longer in the mornings. This is quite normal but not always possible with school.

You can't ask school to start later, but there are some things you can do to help you cope with this body clock change. Try and stick to a routine, going to bed and getting up at the same time. Try not to sleep during the day (at weekends, obviously!). If you feel tired during the day, try doing some exercise. This will energise you physically, make you feel more alert and help you to sleep better later.

Serious stuff

In extreme cases, sleeping too much can be a sign of depression. If you want to sleep all the time, feel sad and withdrawn and avoid being with other people, these could be early signs that you may need to talk to a doctor about how you feel. Don't be embarrassed or ashamed to talk to your parents or carers about how you feel — depression affects people in many different ways.

WHAT'S SO GOOD ABOUT EXERCISE?

Exercise is not only good for your physical well-being but for your mental health too.

Run happy

Exercise releases chemicals into the body, such as endorphins, serotonin and dopamine. These are all the body's natural painkillers that work together to make us feel good. They can actually relieve physical pain and also help to overcome mild depression, anxiety and stress. The best type of exercise to help keep your body strong and make you feel good is cardiovascular exercise. This is exercise, such as jogging, fast cycling or any sport that makes your heart pump faster and makes you feel warmer and breathe faster.

Energetic exercise also reduces the amount of cortisol hormone in your body. Cortisol can be caused by feelings of stress and anxiety that can damage your body and can set up problems for your future health.

sit happy
Other types of exercise are also good for you. Yoga and stretching help to keep your body supple and help to balance your body and mind. This type of exercise can help by clearing away worries and tension and leave you feeling relaxed, calm and refreshed.

Keep moving

Any form of movement is good for you. Dancing, helping with housework, cleaning the car or taking the dog for a walk are all great ways to keep your body moving. You should avoid sitting in the same position for long stretches at a time watching TV or at your computer screen. Stand up, stretch, fetch yourself a glass of water or offer to help make the tea.

39

> Mum was always telling me to get off the sofa but I couldn't be bothered. I liked watching TV and being on my mobile texting mates. I used to feel sleepy all the time and felt bored and fed up. Then a friend suggested we join a local hip-hop dance group. It's brilliant. I have made loads of new friends. I feel stronger and fitter. I'm buzzing with energy the whole time and just feel so much better. It's the best thing I ever did.
>
> Samira, 12

BE POSITIVE!

As we've seen, your thoughts affect how you feel mentally and physically, so try and be positive.

What is being positive?

Being positive is when you expect things to work out for the best. You expect to do well in the English exam and win the football match. Being positive alone won't mean you'll achieve your goals; you need to work for them as well. But if you revise for your English exam or train for a football match believing you will do your best, you are much more likely to enjoy the experience and do well than if you convince yourself you are useless at English and can't kick a football properly.

Being positive also means that if we fail, or don't do as well as we had hoped, we have the motivation to try again and do better next time. It means not being too hard on yourself when something goes wrong, accepting that you tried your best and are prepared to have another go.

All-round benefits

If you work on being positive you will feel better about yourself and your life. This will help your self-esteem and in turn good self-esteem will help you to remain positive. Being positive makes you feel happier and more fun to be around. This is great both for you and your friends and family. Being positive affects you physically too, so you might find you have more energy and enthusiasm to do stuff and try new things.

Down times

We can't be happy, bright and smiley all the time. Everyone has some sad, disappointing and bad times and it is important to accept this. It makes us appreciate the good times all the more and means we are able to understand others who may be having a difficult time themselves. If you are going through a bad time, accept what has happened. It is good to cry and feel sad and even be angry if you need to. Talk to people you can trust about how you feel, write down your feelings, eat well, exercise and remember that whatever you are feeling will get better.

42

"I always struggled with history at school but I really wanted to do well in my exams. My dad told me about visualising doing well – seeing myself succeed. I made sure I did all my revision and homework but every evening I spent 10 minutes seeing myself getting good results and thinking about how great I would feel. I passed! And I felt as good as I thought I would!"

Terri, 14

A HEALTHY FUTURE

Getting into good habits now will keep you mentally and physically healthy as you grow up and become an adult.

43

Good habits

How you treat your body now will affect it for the rest of your life. Having a balanced diet and making sure you sleep well and exercise will help you to cope physically and mentally with school, growing up and life as an adult. If you get into good habits now, you will probably keep them forever.

Bad habits

It's tempting when you're young to try different things, even things that you know are bad for you. Friends can put pressure on you to smoke or drink, for example. They might say you're being pathetic or not one of them if you don't. Both smoking and drinking alcohol can severely damage your health physically and mentally and set up bad habits that you may never be able to change. Say no to smoking and drinking alcohol. Both can make you feel sick, make you smell, make your skin wrinkle and age, ruin your teeth, and will probably shorten your life. And they cost a lot of money. There really isn't a good reason to do either!

Weight aware

More and more adults and children are obese, or very overweight. Being this overweight can damage your health now and into the future. People who are very overweight are more likely to suffer from high blood pressure, diabetes, asthma, arthritis and heart disease as an adult.

If you are worried about being overweight, speak to a trusted adult and ask to see a doctor who will give you advice about healthy eating. No matter how much you weigh don't be tempted to go on a quick-weight-loss diet. Get medical advice, find out what your ideal weight is and lose weight properly.

Mental impact

Whatever we do to our body will affect us mentally. Smoking, drinking alcohol, and eating too much sugary, fatty food will all affect the way we feel. They can make our bodies feel sluggish, our brains foggy and can affect how the brain develops. They can affect how we think and our decision-making. For example, people are more likely to make harmful choices if they have been drinking alcohol.

ONE MORE WORD - MINDFULNESS!

You might have heard
this word a lot, but what
is mindfulness exactly?

Being aware

Mindfulness is being aware of what is happening to us, of how we are feeling physically and mentally. It is knowing what we're thinking and how we're feeling at this moment in time. Stop now and think about it. How does your body feel — tired, energised, twitchy, stiff? How do you feel — bored, interested, sad, angry? What are you thinking — what's for lunch, what am I doing later, will I see my friends tonight?

46

Mental health

By being aware of ourselves more we can notice when we feel stressed or anxious, happy or nervous. This can help us to control those feelings. For example, if you're feeling nervous about taking an exam you can start to breathe slowly and deeply to calm yourself down. Mindfulness makes us think about how we feel right now, and helps us to stop worrying about what might happen in 10 minutes' time.

How to be mindful

Try to become more aware of things going on around you as you walk to school, talk with friends in the playground, go shopping or have a meal with your family. Think about how you feel and how your body feels. If a negative thought comes along, face it. Say: "I feel anxious about the test." Naming your thoughts and facing them may actually make them feel less scary. Not everyone gets on with mindfulness and if it's not for you don't worry about it, at least you've tried.

47

YOUR EMOTIONS

BEING AWARE OF YOUR EMOTIONS HELPS YOU TO UNDERSTAND YOURSELF BETTER, GIVING YOU THE ABILITY TO MAKE GOOD DECISIONS AND BUILD GOOD FRIENDSHIPS. FIND OUT HOW TO HANDLE DIFFICULT EMOTIONS, SUCH AS FEAR AND ANGER, AND HOW TO MAKE THE MOST OF THE EMOTIONS THAT WILL HELP YOU TO BE YOUR BEST YOU.

WHAT ARE EMOTIONS?

We all have emotions that can be positive and negative. But what are emotions exactly?

How are you feeling?

Take a few seconds to think about the way you're feeling right now. You might say that you feel:

Happy

bored

Angry

afraid

EXCITED

lonely

sad

These are all emotions. Often we feel a mix of several different emotions at the same time; perhaps we're excited about something that's going to happen, but a little scared as well because it's something new. Maybe we are angry at something a friend did or said, and sad and disappointed that they upset us. Emotions are the feelings we have about the world around us. People, places, school, home, books, films, music, food, clothes, YouTube videos, Instagram, Facebook — everything that is a part of our lives creates an emotion.

51

Sometimes nice, sometimes nasty

Emotions can be lovely. They can make us feel that the world is a wonderful place. They can make us smile and laugh, feel warm and fuzzy inside and dance for joy.

But some emotions can make us feel dark and nasty and mean. Sometimes our emotions become overwhelming and we feel we can't control them. They can make us want to do bad things to ourselves or others. They can make us feel that the world is a horrible place and that life is unfair.

Learning journey

Often we can get really confused about how we feel. This is normal as we grow up and have new experiences. As we get older, we learn how different experiences affect us and why we feel good or bad about what other people say or do. We learn how to manage negative emotions and how to express our feelings.

Understanding our emotions can help us to manage our feelings properly. This can help us to make good decisions in life, to control our behaviour and build strong relationships with the people around us. Learning about our emotions and why we feel them can be a really rewarding journey.

EMOTIONAL CHAOS

You've probably heard of puberty and how it affects your body. Well, it can affect your mind as well!

Hormones and their effects

As you grow up, and especially when you go through puberty and adolescence, your body changes physically — but so does your mind. Hormones released into your body influence how you feel as well as how you grow. These hormones can affect your emotions, and this can lead to extremes of mood and mood swings. One minute you feel that life is awesome, and the next that it couldn't get any worse!

During puberty your body is dealing with a lot of different physical changes that can make you feel weird or embarrassed. Everyone goes through puberty in their own way. However, if you think your friends might be changing faster or slower than you, this can be frustrating and make you feel 'different' and a bit like an outsider.

Worrying thoughts

When you go through mood swings you can find yourself fighting with family and friends without really knowing why. You might suddenly feel that no one understands you; this can make you feel alone and rejected. You might even feel that you are going mad, because your mind is whirling with thoughts and feelings that you don't understand and can't control.

55

It's not just you

Feeling like this can be very scary and even though it's your hormones causing havoc, you have to find a way to manage your feelings. Remember that *everyone*, including your teachers, parents and carers, went through something similar at the same age. If you feel really confused and anxious about how you feel, talk to someone. You could speak to an adult you trust at home or at school, or even see a doctor who can reassure you.

WHAT ELSE AFFECTS MOODS?

Of course it's not just hormones that affect how we feel. Big and little everyday experiences will cause us to feel different emotions.

People power

The people around us can affect how we feel. Being with friends and family who love and support us makes us feel happy and confident. If we're with people who make us feel weak and stupid, then we will feel bad about ourselves. Sometimes social media can make us feel sad and lonely and jealous when we see others having a fun time with loads of friends.

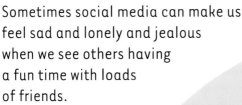

Lifestyle

What we eat, how well we sleep and how much exercise we do all affect our moods. Experts say you should try to get at least nine to ten hours' sleep a night and eat well. Try to avoid too much sugar and fizzy drinks. Keep yourself hydrated by drinking lots of water throughout the day. If you become dehydrated it can make you feel more grumpy.

Exercise is important, too. It releases feel-good hormones into the body that make us feel better and help to release stress and tension in the body. Even just having a good stretch and jogging on the spot for a few minutes will help relax your body.

Trauma

Sometimes very sad things happen. Someone we love dies, or the family splits up, or someone we care about becomes ill. This will be a difficult time for everyone, but especially for young people already being affected by puberty. If something like this happens to you, talk to a teacher, an adult you know well and trust or phone a helpline (see pages 172–174).

You could write down your feelings in a journal or write a poem or a song about how you feel. People often feel angry with a loved one who has died, become ill or left the family — this is a natural reaction and is nothing to feel ashamed of.

> When Dad left us I was angry with everyone. I blamed Mum, then I blamed Dad. Then I thought it was my fault; I was so confused and scared and sad. Eventually I talked to another girl in my class who was going through the same thing and felt the same way. We both felt better for talking. I'm still sad but I don't feel so alone and scared anymore.
>
> **Steph, 11**

58

EMOTIONS AND THOUGHTS

Your thoughts can control how you feel so you need to be aware of them.

Thought power

Our brain is filled with thoughts that can affect how we feel. Here are some positive thoughts:

I'm really good at maths!

I'm excited about joining the drama group.

My skin looks great today.

Positive thoughts like this help us to feel happy and full of energy. They help us to feel good about ourselves.

Now look at these negative thoughts:

I'm useless at maths.

Nobody in the drama group will think I'm any good.

My skin looks awful.

Negative thoughts make us feel sad and anxious and bad about ourselves.

60

From bad to worse

Sometimes people say things that set up a negative thought that grows and grows. For example, your dad might jokingly say that you can't kick a football straight. This grows in your mind to become 'you're useless at football' and 'I'm really disappointed in you'. These negative thoughts have a bad effect on your self-esteem, or how you see yourself. Before you know it, you're convinced you're useless at everything and worthless.

Train your brain

You'll need to be patient, but you can train your brain to be positive. Make a list of all the things you and other people like about you – being kind, good at swimming, and so on. Stick it up in your room where you can see it. When you're feeling bad about yourself, look at your 'likes' list. If you find it hard to shake off your negative feelings, talk to a trusted adult and maybe see a doctor to have a chat about it.

61

> " My older sister was always teasing me about my hair saying it was wild and looked a mess. It made me feel awful – I thought everyone was looking at my hair and laughing. I asked my mum if I could cut it all off and we had a long talk about how I felt. She spoke to my sister who had no idea how I felt and said she was sorry she'd upset me. She said she thought I had very pretty hair. I felt much better and started wearing combs and clips in my hair to show it off.

Aisha, 10

"

EMOTIONS AND BEHAVIOUR

Our emotions control how we behave, what we do and say, and how we feel about ourselves and the world around us.

Why have emotions?

Emotions play an important part in how we behave in our everyday lives. They affect the decisions we make, how well we do at school and how we treat our family and friends.

62

Emotions can make us feel good or bad. Sadness, boredom, anger and fear make us feel bad, so we try to avoid them. Happiness, excitement and love make us feel good, so we look for them.

This affects our decision-making and behaviour, as generally we do things to make ourselves and others feel good rather than bad. For example, when we do something that makes someone we care about sad or disappointed we feel guilty. We even feel guilty when we make ourselves feel bad, for example, by not doing our homework or by being mean to someone. To avoid feeling guilty again, we do our homework and we're careful not to be mean to anyone. As a result, our dislike of feeling bad has made us behave in a good way.

63

Emotional awareness

As we grow up and experience different situations we begin to get better at knowing how ourselves and others are feeling and why. This is called emotional awareness. Being more aware of how we feel and why, helps to develop emotional intelligence. This is an important skill that we will use all our lives.

To develop a healthy emotional awareness you need to be aware of the emotions you feel, and remember when and why you felt them and how you reacted. For example, does a certain song or book make you feel relaxed and inspired or bored and sad? Does being with your friends make you feel happy and excited, or anxious and nervous? By monitoring your feelings you can decide what is good or bad in your life and make changes when you need to.

Get to know your emotions

Talk about your feelings to your friends, family, or even your pet, or write about them in a feelings journal. This helps you to express your emotions and to find the words to explain them to yourself and to other people. Don't be afraid of emotions such as anger, frustration, jealousy and fear.

Talking honestly about your emotions and thinking about how and why you are feeling one way or another can help you to manage these feelings in the future.

SWEATY PALMS AND A RED FACE!

Anxiety and strong emotions, such as anger and fear, can have a physical effect.

Adrenaline surge

Some stressful situations, such as playing in a football match or taking an exam, can make some people feel sick or light-headed. This is because stress causes a hormone called adrenaline to be pumped around your body.

Adrenaline is released into the body when we feel scared, threatened or very anxious. It is also called the 'fight-or-flight' hormone because it prepares the body to either fight the real or imagined threat or run and escape from it. It does this by contracting blood vessels, making the heart beat faster, restricting air passages and sometimes making you want to go to the loo a lot! Once the scare is over, the adrenaline levels return to normal.

Sweaty palms

Lots of people get sweaty palms when they feel anxious or nervous. It often happens if you feel shy or embarrassed in front of other people. It is part of the adrenaline fight-or-flight response to a threatening situation and is perfectly normal. There can also be medical reasons why some people sweat too much. If excessive sweating is stopping you from joining in games, affecting your daily life or making you feel anxious, speak to your parents or carers and ask to see a doctor. If it is being caused by anxiety, it will help to talk to someone about why you are feeling so anxious.

Red face

Suddenly blushing, flushing or getting pink or red cheeks is often caused by, yes, you guessed it, adrenaline! Talking to new people or standing in front of an audience makes lots of people feel anxious or nervous. This creates an adrenaline surge that makes blood rush to the face, causing blushing.

When we meet new people we want them to like us and so subconsciously we are thinking about what impression we are making. This feeling of nervousness can cause us to blush.

TRY THIS!

Next time you are in a situation that makes you blush, take a deep breath and breathe out slowly. Focus on the people you are talking to and what you think about them. That way you'll stop thinking about yourself.

FEELING SAD

Everyone feels sad at times and it's perfectly normal to have sad feelings.

What makes us feel sad?

Some things in life make us sad, from a weepy film, or a good friend moving away, to something really big like the death of a relative or a family break-up. Some sad feelings only last for a short time, while others can be very painful and last for a very long time.

Sadness can also make us feel lonely. It can isolate us from other people who are having a good time and make us feel alone.

In most cases we can do things to help us to feel better when we are sad, but sometimes the sadness is just too great and can be overwhelming. Talk to someone about why you feel so sad. It might help to have a good cry. Keep a journal about your sadness – but don't share what you write online. Keep these personal thoughts private. Drawing and painting can sometimes help us to express our sadness especially when we can't talk about it. Even the worst sadness you can think of gets easier to cope with over time.

How to cope

Learning to understand and manage your emotions is part of becoming an adult. For example, if you've done badly in an exam you can choose to learn from what went wrong and be determined to do better next time.

If one of your friends doesn't want to talk to you any more, see it as their loss and look for other friends that you can trust, or join a new club to do more of a hobby you enjoy. Disappointment and failure can make you feel sad, but can also be opportunities to try something new and be better.

Depression

There are different levels of sadness and sometimes feeling sad can become something more serious that needs medical help. If you feel sad for a long time, feel irritable and grumpy all the time, lose interest in being with your friends, can't be bothered with schoolwork, sleep more or can't sleep at all, feel tired and exhausted and have thoughts about harming yourself, you may be suffering from depression. Speak to your parents or carers and ask to see your doctor who will give you professional advice. Don't leave it and hope it will go away; ask for help.

FEELING HAPPY

We all want to be happy
and often it is the smallest things
that make us truly content.

Can't buy happiness

It sounds boring, but it's true: you can't buy happiness.
It might make you feel good when you buy a new pair of
trainers or the latest video game, but the feeling doesn't
last. Scientific research has shown that shopping releases
feel-good hormones into the brain, but this feeling only
lasts for a short while. You then have to buy something else
to feel the same way again.

Feeling truly happy comes from how you live your life, how you treat others and how you feel about yourself and the world. Being with people you love and who love you back, being kind, caring and having people care for you, are the things that make us truly content.

Make yourself happy

Most of the time, unless there's a medical reason why you feel sad (see page 70), you have the power to make yourself happy. It hurts when people are mean to you and it is disappointing if you can't buy what you really want, but you can control how you deal with these emotions.

You can believe the mean things people say or you can ignore them and walk away. You can feel angry and upset that you can't buy what you want, or you can think of ways to make some extra pocket money so that you can save up to buy it. Taking control of your emotions and behaving in a positive way helps to make you feel strong and increases your self-esteem, which makes you feel good about yourself and happy!

Friends!

Having good friends helps to keep us feeling positive and stops us feeling sad and lonely. Good friends are kind, respectful and loyal. And remember, being 'popular' isn't the same as having good friends. Having one or two really close friends that you trust is worth more than having lots of friends who hang around with you but don't really care about you.

"

When my mum and dad split up I was so angry and scared. I was really mean to my best mate, but he knew what was going on at home and stood by me. One day we were playing football and I blurted out how I felt. I still don't know what's going to happen, but I feel a lot better knowing my mate is there for me and that he's not judging me.

Ryan, 14

"

FEELING ANGRY

We all feel angry at times and that's fine; it's how we deal with our anger that's important.

Aargh!

There are lots of reasons why we feel angry. It could be when someone says something that is wrong or mean. Or it could be when you think that life is being unfair. Maybe you feel angry when you want to do something and your parents say 'no', or when you try to learn something new and struggle to get it right.

Some anger is good, for example, if someone is being bullied at school it is right to get angry and tell a teacher. It's how we behave when we're dealing with feelings of anger that's important.

Deal with it

Try and deal calmly with what made you angry or hurt you. Speak to the person who upset you or if you feel frustrated with schoolwork, talk to a teacher about it. At home, think about what makes you angry, but instead of expressing your frustration, ask the adults for a time when you can sit down and talk when they can give you their full attention. Tell them calmly why you feel angry and then listen to what they say to you.

See if you can solve the issues in a grown-up way that will make you all feel better about the situation.

Don't lose it!

Sometimes stress about school or home can build up until we feel like exploding. If you feel like this, try not to shout, scream, be abusive or lash out. Losing your temper and being aggressive or violent will only make any situation much, much worse. If you can, walk away from what has made you angry. Find somewhere quiet — in the garden, an empty classroom — anywhere that is a safe space. Take deep breaths and slowly count to 10. If you can, punch a pillow, scream into a cushion, stamp your feet and clench and unclench your fists.

Don't be a bully

If you are taking your anger out on other people by bullying or being nasty, think about why you are angry. If someone is bullying you or making you feel ashamed or bad about yourself, you need to talk to someone you trust about it. Taking your anger out on other people will only make you feel worse about yourself and could get you into trouble.

FEELING SCARED

Everyone feels scared sometimes and this is not necessarily a bad thing. Fear can be a destructive emotion, but it can be useful, too.

Feeling fear

We feel afraid when we don't know what's going to happen or when we think something bad is going happen. We should listen to our fear when it is a warning not to do something dangerous, but how can we deal with fear when it stops us doing things that might be good for us?

Afraid to fail

A fear of failure means we avoid trying new things in case we don't get them right or make a fool of ourselves trying. Everyone feels like this sometimes, even adults, and the truth is that some of the most successful people in the world, from singers to business billionaires, have made plenty of mistakes along the way. If we do our best but still fail it can be a good thing. Failing teaches us the right way to do something or to try a different way. We can all learn from failure. When you do fail don't think you're a loser and useless, think positive thoughts about how you can make it work next time.

Anxiety

Anxiety is when you feel worried, nervous and scared to try something because you don't know what might happen. It could be meeting new people or sitting an exam, for example. When you get anxious you might be aware of a fluttery feeling in your tummy, your heart might beat faster and you might start to sweat more. Remember everyone gets anxious at times, so it's not just you.

From fear to phobia

Sometimes a fear we have can develop into something more serious. A phobia is when a person becomes too terrified to do something, for example, being afraid to leave their home in case something terrible happens to them outside.

If you have a phobia that is affecting your day-to-day life, talk to an adult you trust about it and seek medical help. A doctor or specialist will be able to help you deal with the phobia. Don't think you're being weak or silly by asking for help; it's a very brave thing to do.

"

My panic attacks started when I was nine. I would shake and sweat and feel like being sick. I couldn't breathe and felt like I was being smothered. My mum took me to see a specialist and it really helped. I am okay at school now and can go out with friends. At last my life is getting back to normal.

Jake, 15

"

RELATIONSHIPS

The relationships we have throughout our lives have a very important effect on how we feel about ourselves and the world around us.

Connections

A relationship is an emotional connection between two or more people. Our first relationships are with our family — the adults who look after us, brothers and sisters, aunts, uncles, grandparents and cousins.

As we get older we start to develop friendships and relationships with people outside the family, such as classmates and teachers. Later, we will have relationships with lots of people, including people we work with. Building caring, supportive relationships throughout our lives is very important to our physical and mental wellbeing.

Mixed emotions

All relationships are based on emotions. The emotions can be positive, such as love, joy and excitement, or negative, such as hate, anger and sadness. Most relationships are a mix of all these emotions. We love and care for our family and friends, but often get angry with them or feel sad if we feel they've let us down.

81

This is completely normal and healthy if we can talk about what has upset us and then move on. In a strong relationship the positive emotions are much stronger than the negative ones and communication between you stays open and honest whatever happens.

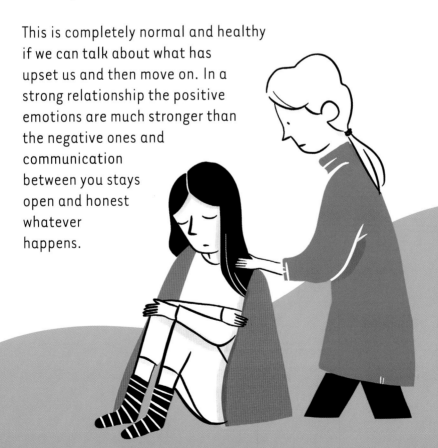

Good feelings

If someone has a caring, loving and supportive family they feel happier, more confident and have higher self-esteem. If their family is always arguing, or being nasty to each other, this makes them feel miserable and can affect their self-esteem and schoolwork. If a sibling or adult at home is making you feel scared or bad about yourself, you don't have to put up with it just because you are a child. Speak to a trusted adult who will be able to help you decide what to do or call a helpline (see pages 172–174). Every child has the right to feel safe and cared for at home.

"

My older sister was really sad because her boyfriend had broken up with her. We haven't always been best friends, but I hated seeing her like that. One day I went and sat with her and held her hand and took her my favourite teddy. We didn't say anything; she just cried and I hugged her. Later she said that made her feel much better and how lucky she was to have such a kind sister. I felt so pleased and proud that I'd been able to help her.

Poppy, 10

"

FRIENDS FOR LIFE

Friends are a very important part of your life so it's important to know how to be a good friend.

A good friend:

• praises and compliments you when you've done something special

• hugs and comforts you when things go wrong

• supports and encourages you to do your best

• listens to you and shares their own feelings with you

• is someone you can trust and rely on to be there for you and who makes you feel happy and good about yourself.

What is empathy?

As young people get older and start to go through puberty, they usually become more aware of how other people feel and react to them. They develop a sense of empathy. Empathy is when we understand and share other people's emotions and feelings. For example, if a friend is having a tough time at home, you can see how sad or angry the friend is. You understand how your friend is feeling even though you aren't feeling that emotion yourself. Because of this you can comfort your friend and try and make them feel better, or just be there for them.

Sometimes your feeling of empathy might be so strong you find that you feel angry for your friend or that their sadness makes you cry. This works with good feelings, too. If a friend has passed an exam or won a sports match, you can feel really happy for them.

Oh, no! Frenemies!

These are the opposite of good friends. They are people who say they are your friend, but they put you down all the time. They laugh if you make a mistake and jeer if you get something right. They can be jealous and nasty.

Everyone deserves to have good friends so take steps to put things right. Talk to the friend who is upsetting you the most. If they are sorry and feel bad about what they've done, you can decide to give them another chance.

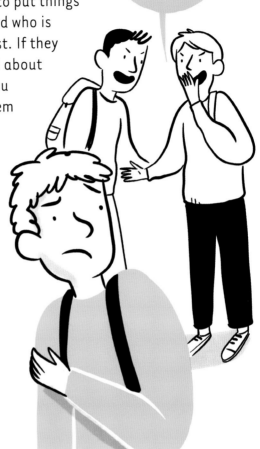

If they laugh and call you names, you need to drop them. They were never true friends at all and you'll be happier finding new friends. This is not easy to do, but it will increase your self-esteem to know that you took steps to make yourself feel better.

Making new friends

Not everyone makes friends easily; we can all feel a bit scared of being rejected or ignored sometimes, but remember, everyone feels the same. Join a club or group to meet people who share the same interests. Sit near a group of people you like or go up to someone sitting alone and say hello to them. You never know, this could be your new best friend!

ONE MORE WORD ... ME!

Be your own best friend
and find out what makes you
feel the best you can.

Know 'me'

Take some time to think about what makes you happy and excited, what you look forward to and who you enjoy being with. Keeping a journal of your feelings can often help to pinpoint what made you feel anxious and worried or joyful and pleased. Once you know what triggers your different emotions, you can do more to encourage the good ones and avoid the bad ones.

Forgive 'me'

We all do and say things we regret, but what is important is what we do about it afterwards. Saying sorry, explaining why you behaved the way you did and making sure not to do it again, is a very grown up and brave thing to do. Above all, forgive yourself. Don't end up feeling guilty about what you did and thinking you're a bad person, and don't allow other people to make you feel guilty. These are negative feelings that can affect your whole outlook, but only if you let them.

Love 'me'

Try to fill your life with as many positive emotions as you can by being caring and kind to others. Make a point to have a go at learning new skills and having new experiences. Believe that you are valuable and worthwhile, and know that you are unique and special and deserve happiness and love.

BEATING STRESS AND ANXIETY

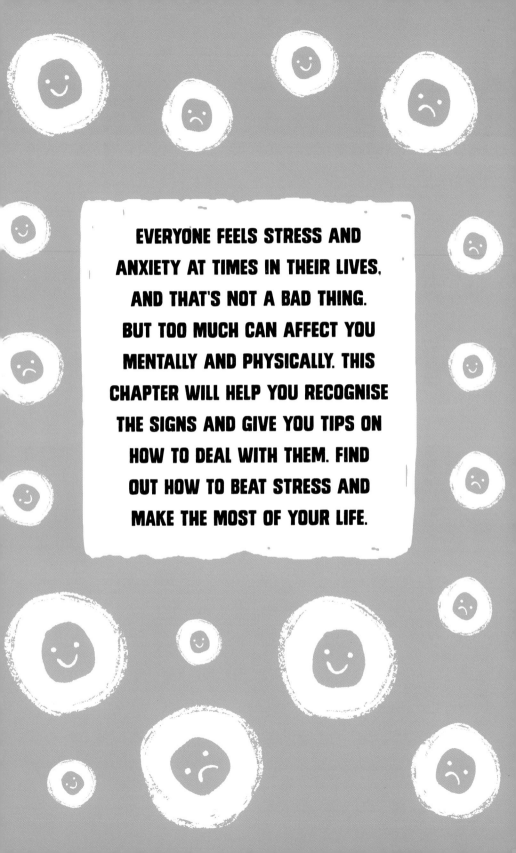

EVERYONE FEELS STRESS AND ANXIETY AT TIMES IN THEIR LIVES, AND THAT'S NOT A BAD THING. BUT TOO MUCH CAN AFFECT YOU MENTALLY AND PHYSICALLY. THIS CHAPTER WILL HELP YOU RECOGNISE THE SIGNS AND GIVE YOU TIPS ON HOW TO DEAL WITH THEM. FIND OUT HOW TO BEAT STRESS AND MAKE THE MOST OF YOUR LIFE.

WHAT IS STRESS?

Everybody experiences stress throughout their lifetime. Normal stress can sometimes be a good thing.

Describing stress

Stress is the feeling you get when you're worried, upset or uncomfortable about something. Stress affects you mentally and physically. It can make you feel sick, make your heart pound, give you a headache and make it difficult to sleep properly. You may feel like going to the loo all the time, start shivering or sweating or feel like your legs have turned to jelly.

Normal stress

We usually feel stressed or worried when something new or important is about to happen, such as starting a new school, taking an exam, trying out a new hobby or making a presentation in front of the class. These feelings are perfectly normal and shouldn't last very long. This kind of stress can help you to focus on what you are doing. It can make you work harder to get your homework done on time or give you the energy to play a better game of football.

Bad stress

If you feel stressed all the time, can't sleep or eat because you are worrying, can't concentrate at school, feel irritable and grumpy and shout at people when you don't mean to, these can be signs that you are badly stressed or are staying stressed for long periods of time.

This kind of bad stress can be caused by a traumatic event such as the death of a loved one or a family breaking up. But it can also be caused by something like constantly worrying over how many likes we have or the comments we're getting on social media. Instead of the stress helping us and then going away, it builds up and can make us feel worse physically and mentally.

STRESS TEST

No one should feel stressed all the time. Think about how stressed you are and why.

Busy lives

Young people have a lot going on in their lives. Going to school, making friends, family life, social media ... it can be fun and exciting, but it can be stressful at times, too. Many young people look after a parent or sibling who isn't well, or have to cope with a family splitting up. Life for adults can also be stressful and this can affect the whole family. When we feel stressed, our brain releases hormones into our body to help cope with the event. If the stress goes on for too long, our body is constantly flooded with these hormones and this can damage our health both physically and mentally.

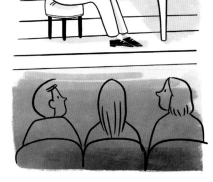

Why stressed?

When you feel stressed, stop and take a few breaths and think about why you feel stressed. If there is one specific thing worrying you, visualise or create a picture in your mind of everything going to plan and ending well. If you can't pinpoint one thing, or there are loads of things, take some time to try and stop the cycle of stress instead of carrying on worrying about it all. Too much stress can affect your health and your schoolwork, and make you feel miserable.

95

> *I heard Mum and Dad talking about money problems. It made me worry that we would have to move house and I would have to find a new school and I'd lose all my friends. I couldn't think of anything else but I didn't want Mum and Dad to know I'd heard. Eventually I told my aunt and she told my parents. They did have some money problems but nothing like as bad as I imagined. I was worrying for nothing!*
>
> Ben, 12

COPING WITH STRESS

There are lots of different ways to cope with stress. First you have to know what's causing the stress.

Take action

If the thing that's making you stressed is something obvious, like an exam or giving a class talk, you can take steps to deal with your stress. Prepare for the event. Do the work required, whether it's practising a talk, researching a subject or revising. Make a list of what needs to be done and organise your time so you get everything done in time and feel that you have control over the event, rather than it having you in a grip of worry. Accept that if it does go wrong, it's not the end of the world, but feel confident that it will all go to plan.

Social media

We can spend a lot of time on social media posting images, commenting and keeping up with our online and real friends. It can be fun but it can also cause stress and worry if we don't get enough likes or shares, or the right sort of comments. We might worry about not being online to accept an invite straightaway, or stress about missing out on something cool that is happening. Social media life can begin to take over, and instead of being fun, becomes a big source of stress.

If this is happening, think about what is making you stressed. Is it not getting enough likes or shares? Why does this worry you? Think about why you need the approval of others. Is it to boost your self-esteem or because of FOMO — fear of missing out?

TRY THIS!

If social media is stressing you out you can decide to have a social media de-stress. No need to stay off social media totally, but try it for a little while, or for a few hours a week just link up online with close friends and family. Check out sites that make you feel happy and relaxed rather than worried and anxious. Arrange to meet up with friends in real life and go for a walk or just sit at home and chat or listen to music. This will give you the space to stop worrying.

98

WHAT IS ANXIETY?

Anxiety is when we are afraid, uneasy or worried about something unknown or uncertain.

Describing anxiety

Anxiety is the feeling of being worried or afraid of what might happen. It is feeling fearful of the unknown, of bad things happening, of the future. Physical symptoms include a racing heart, feeling faint, running to the loo, being tired and irritable, unable to sleep or concentrate, having bad dreams and losing your appetite.

As we've seen, these symptoms can be as a result of stress, and everyone will experience some of them at some time. But if you have symptoms like these for a week or so and they are affecting your schoolwork and stopping you from enjoying life, you should talk to a trusted adult. It might also help to see your doctor.

Major changes

Going to a new school when you move home or when you transfer from primary to secondary school is a huge change for young people and can make them feel very anxious. Try thinking about it as a new adventure. Yes, it is a bit scary, but in an exciting way. Be positive and open about what the new school holds and look forward to the challenge. If it all seems a bit overwhelming, talk to someone you trust or phone a helpline (see pages 172–174). It may not seem important enough to bother anyone, but if it is making you anxious and scared, then you should talk to someone about it.

Big and bad

Sometimes, sadly, terrible things happen. Someone dies or becomes very ill, a family splits up or life changes in some other way that is painful. When something this big happens we need to talk about our feelings, rather than bottling them up and putting on a brave face. It is perfectly okay and natural to feel sad and cry.

101

Sometimes a big life trauma can make us feel out of control and make us worry about other bad things that might happen in the future. This is natural and it will help to talk to someone about how you feel. Don't feel ashamed or embarrassed about feeling sad or afraid — it is completely normal to feel this way.

WHAT IF ...?

There are different forms of thinking that can make us feel stressed and anxious.

I can tell the future

No one can say what the future holds but that doesn't stop us worrying about what might happen. Some people who feel anxious think that the worst will happen, so they predict the exam will be an absolute failure, no one at the new school will like them and they will have a miserable life. Oh dear, that's a lot to worry about.

It will be amazing – or awful

This is when you convince yourself that the outcome of something will be either brilliant or a disaster. So the exam will be a total triumph or a complete failure. The pizza you're making will be the best ever or absolutely disgusting. The truth is, most things are never that extreme.

I know what people think

This is when you think you know what people are thinking or are going to think about you. You know they will think you are stupid, laugh at your hair, hate your clothes and talk about you behind you back. You have no reason to think this, and everyone might be being very nice, but you have it stuck in your mind that this is what is going on.

Think again

If you catch yourself thinking in any of these ways, stop and have a rethink. How do you know things will go badly? Is it really realistic to think in these extreme terms? And if you do fail the exam or your pizza isn't the best ever, is that really the end of the world? Even if things don't go as well as you had hoped, there will be other chances to try again and do better.

Overthinking

Overthinking is when you think or obsess about all the tiny details of something non-stop, looking for different meanings or reasons. Or when you worry about small details after the event, such as what you said/should have said/didn't say/could have said. Argh! Social media can be particularly stressful as you worry about what to write, why no one's 'liked' you, whether you wrote the wrong thing, whether people misunderstood what you wrote, whether you should rewrite it, on and on ... it's exhausting!
Stop, now!

Think about something else that is fun and positive. Read a book, listen to your favourite music, do some exercise. If you let your thoughts swirl about in your head, they will just go on and on, making you feel more and more wound up, so make a choice to stop them and take control.

GOOD THINKING!

Everyone has times when they think the world is against them or that they are useless, but you can change the way you think.

Here's a situation ...

Imagine you've taken a science test. Your teacher says you thought through the answers well, but unfortunately you failed the test because you got some facts wrong.

How would you feel?

A

It would have been good to pass but at least you got some positive feedback. You can do some extra research into the facts you didn't know.

B

You are useless at science and probably everything else as well.

If you chose B, you are forgetting or filtering out all the positive things people say about you and that you know about yourself. This is very common and lots of people do it. We remember the bad or negative things people say about us rather than the good, positive things. If you believe you are rubbish at science, that fact you failed the test will support this. You will forget that you actually did some good work in the test.

Don't forget the good stuff

When you start to have negative thoughts about yourself, take a deep breath, sit in a quiet space and think it through. Are you really that bad at science? If you are, why did your teacher say you gave some good answers? Think about how you can do better next time. Feel good that you got some positive feedback and make a plan to do better next time.

Online social stress

On social media you may get some nasty comments, or not enough comments or 'likes', or people may suddenly block you for no reason or leave you out of invites and messages. Don't think it is all your fault and that you must have done something wrong. People do things for reasons we don't always understand. Block the person that is upsetting you or switch off the blog that makes you feel bad about yourself. Your time on social media should be fun, creative and supportive.

TRY THIS!

Keep a diary or memory jar of all the positive and good things that happen to you, like scoring a goal in football, mastering a dance move, someone giving you a compliment, suddenly understanding a maths problem, getting a good mark for your essay, making a new friend. When you feel negative or bad about yourself, take a look through your diary or pull out some memories from the jar and remember the positive things.

STRESS AT HOME

Your home should be a safe, happy place but every family has times when they go through a bad patch or difficult experiences.

Family arguments

All families have disagreements and arguments. Adults and children get cross with each other but they soon make it up. Sometimes, though, the arguments can get nasty, especially between adults. Perhaps rows get longer and louder, the adults throw things or even hurt each other. If this is happening in your home or you feel scared, anxious and unsafe there, you must tell a trusted adult. You are not telling tales; it is your right to feel safe. And sometimes, if another person steps in, it can help solve the problems that are causing the arguments.

108

Not good enough

Most parents and carers only want what is best for their children, but sometimes this means they push them to achieve the top results, to go to the best university or to excel at a subject such as maths or sport. This puts a lot of pressure on young people to succeed to please their family.

It can cause them added worry and anxiety, especially if they are not as successful as their parents would wish. If you feel this pressure, talk to the people it's coming from. Try and explain that you are doing your best. If it is the case, explain that the constant pressure of always having to succeed can make it difficult to sleep properly or concentrate on schoolwork, so it has the opposite effect.

Feeling safe

Your home should be a safe place and your family safe
people to be with, but this isn't always the case. No matter
how difficult life is at home, usually children continue to
love their family and don't want to get them into trouble.
But suffering high levels of stress and anxiety as a young
person can affect someone for the rest of their life. Stress
releases chemicals into the body that can be linked to
illness later in life.

Mentally, constant stress and worry can cause depression,
feelings of worthlessness and isolation and lead
to self-harm and even thoughts of suicide. If you are
feeling threatened, anxious or scared at home you must
speak to a trusted adult or phone a helpline (see pages
172–174).

MAKING FRIENDS

Social events should be fun, but many people find they make them feel stressed and anxious.

Meeting new people

Being anxious about meeting new people and being in new situations is normal. Remember that most other people are feeling the same as you. Smile, say "hi" and be friendly. Listen to what people have to say and ask questions without asking anything too personal. Keep in mind that not everyone will instantly get on and become best mates, and we can't be friends with everyone. If you don't feel a connection with someone, don't force it or change to try and fit in with other people.

Deep breaths

Some people start to blush when they feel anxious. They might even begin to sweat or stammer. This happens to lots of people and is nothing to worry about. The more you think about it the worse it will feel. You probably notice it a lot more than anyone else. Take deep breaths before a stressful situation, and be determined to make the best of it, whether it's taking a test or joining a new club.

Being judged

Some people feel very anxious and scared about meeting new people or talking in front of a group because they believe that they are being judged. They think they will do something silly and make a fool of themselves and be laughed at. This makes them feel even more anxious and might stop them doing things such as joining new groups and clubs and making friends.

If your anxiety about meeting new people or talking in front of a group is making you feel ill or stopping you making friends, you need to talk to someone you trust about it, either face-to-face or via a phone helpline. Feeling this way is nothing to be embarrassed about and it is not being silly. There are lots of ways that a doctor or specialists can help people overcome these feelings of anxiety.

How do I look?

Are you anxious about how you look or worried whether people will think you look okay and want to be your friend? Remember we can't all look and be the same. You are you, a special and unique person and you don't need to change yourself to fit in with a group or crowd. Be friendly and kind to other people. Be proud of your own style and looks. Find friends who like you for who you are.

113

> When a new dance class started locally I was really excited about joining. But when the day came I felt really anxious. I thought everyone else would be great dancers and I would make a fool of myself! Walking into the room my knees went to jelly and my heart started beating really fast. I almost turned around and left but felt determined to give it a try. I'm pleased I did. Everyone was very friendly and I'm loving learning the dance routines and making new friends.
>
> Lina, 12

PANIC ATTACKS

Panic attacks can happen to anyone at any time, but what are they and why do they happen?

The signs of a panic attack

A person who is having a panic attack can experience breathlessness, a feeling that something terrible is going to happen, feeling sick, dizziness, a fast-beating heart, a feeling of choking and feeling very hot or very cold. An attack can be caused by a number of different things. If someone has had a panic attack they may get stressed about having another one.

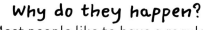

Why do they happen?

Most people like to have a regular routine where they know what is going to happen and what is expected of them. When this routine changes, it can make us feel anxious. For young people there are lots of changes in life, such as starting new schools and making new friends. This can increase anxiety and worry, and trigger something like a panic attack.

Avoiding attacks

When someone has a panic attack, it is very natural for them to avoid doing whatever it was that caused the panic attack in the first place. So, whether it's going through a tunnel or joining a new group or club where you don't know anyone, the thought of doing those things again will be terrifying and the person will do everything possible to avoid them.

The best way to overcome the fear is to do the same thing again. You can do this with someone you trust. Or you can ask your doctor for specialist help. Remember no one dies from panic attacks and they do not mean that there is anything physically wrong with you.

TRY THIS!

If you ever have a panic attack, find an adult and tell them what is happening. Breathe slowly. Look at your favourite photos on your phone to take your mind off what is happening. Call a friend or family member, someone you trust, that you can talk to until you feel better. Panic attacks are very scary but they only last about 10 minutes, although it can seem like forever if you're having one.

ROUTINES AND RITUALS

Everyone has little routines they do to help with stress, but sometimes these can grow to become an obsession.

Ways of coping

When we are anxious or worried we do lots of little things to help us cope, and sometimes we don't even know we're doing them. For example, if you're going out for the day, your mum or dad might check more than once to make sure they've got the car keys or that the back door is locked, even though they already know the keys are in their bag and all the doors are safely locked! Maybe you hum, or tap a pencil or count to 100 to cope when you are feeling stressed. These small routines are harmless and can be very soothing and reassuring in stressful situations.

Keeping the bad away

Sometimes these little routines or rituals can turn into an obsession. This is when a person feels they have to do them to stop something really bad happening. If they can't, they become scared and anxious, and might have signs of a panic attack. Sometimes this is called Obsessive Compulsive Disorder (OCD). Scientists don't really know yet what causes it.

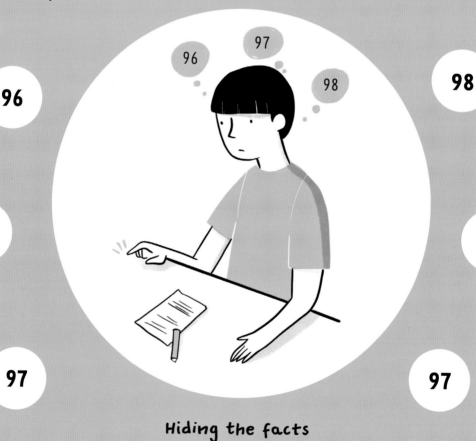

Hiding the facts

Young people who have irrational fears and behave in this way sometimes feel too embarrassed or ashamed to talk to anyone about it. They try to hide their rituals from friends and family in case they are teased or laughed at.

If you think you may have OCD or if your routines are stopping you doing things or upsetting your home or school life, you need to speak to your adults at home about it. There are lots of different ways that doctors can help with OCD so there is no need to suffer alone.

119

> *It started when I was 11. I became anxious that someone in my family would become really ill and I worried about germs killing us. I had to wash my hands all the time. I spent ages washing before bed and when I came home from being outside I would wash and rewash my hands and arms in case I brought germs into the house. Mum took me to see a doctor who understood why I felt so anxious. He suggested some therapy. You have to work out why you feel so anxious and find ways to control it. It's hard work but I'm much better now.*

Jeffrey, 13

HELP AT HOME

If you're feeling anxious
or worried you need to talk to
people at home about it.

Don't feel embarrassed

You may feel embarrassed or silly talking to your parents
or carers about your anxiety or worries. Maybe you feel
that you should be able to cope, especially if you have
siblings or friends who are managing school, homework,
friends, joining clubs and passing exams. But everyone is
different so don't feel that just because everyone else is
coping, you should be able to as well.

120

We all need help sometimes and it is your parents' or carers' job to look after you and help you when things get difficult. It is very grown up to recognise that you need help and to ask for it. The sooner you ask for help the sooner you'll start to feel better.

Where to start

Choose a quiet time to talk about your worries. Rather than saying something out of the blue over dinner or when they are rushing to get to work in the morning, tell your parents or carers you want to talk and ask them to set a time when they can give you their full attention. Everyone needs to be calm and focused, including you.

121

If talking face-to-face is making you feel more anxious, write your worries down in a letter and ask your parents or carers to read it when they have some quiet time.

Be truthful

Be as honest as you can about how you feel. Explain that you feel anxious and it is making you feel sick and scared, or you worry all the time about being asked to read in front of the class or whatever it is that is troubling you. They may say that you'll grow out of it, or that it will get better or to keep on trying.

If you feel your parents or carers don't fully understand, call a helpline (see pages 172–174) and ask for advice on how to speak to them or speak to a trusted family member or a teacher about how you feel.

I spoke to my dad when I was feeling really anxious about giving a class talk. Just the thought was making me feel sick. Dad noticed that I was quiet and spent a lot of time in my room, so when he asked what was wrong, we sat down and had a chat. He understood more than I thought he would – said he used to feel anxious about talking in front of people as well. Just talking to him and knowing he understood really helped a lot.

Sam, 11

ENJOY LIFE

A healthy diet, having fun, exercising and getting a good night's sleep will all help you to keep stress and anxiety under control.

Good diet, feel good

How you look after your body affects how you think and feel. Nutrients such as vitamins and minerals in fruit, vegetables, fish and carbohydrates help to keep your brain working and growing well. They help you to concentrate on your schoolwork and improve your memory, as well as helping you to cope with mood swings and feeling down. Eating too much sugary food will make you feel sluggish and slow physically and mentally. Keep sweet things as a special treat every now and then.

Exercise — it works!

Exercise releases chemicals called endorphins into your brain. These endorphins help to make you feel happy and good about yourself. When you do any exercise that makes your heart beat faster you pump more oxygen around your body. Oxygen keeps your brain in good working order and helps to keep you feeling alert.

Exercise also keeps you fit so you feel good about your body. When you feel good physically, this helps you to cope with worries and anxiety.

Zzzzz

A good night's sleep helps you to concentrate and cope with challenges. Not getting enough sleep can make you feel grumpy and not able to focus on schoolwork. Lack of sleep might also make you feel physically tired so you won't be able to play games as well as you might and you won't enjoy being with your friends as much as you usually do.

Friends and family

Being with good friends or family, having fun, chatting and laughing, reading a brilliant book or watching your favourite film, sharing your day with people you love and who care about you and doing activities that make you feel excited. All these things help you to feel relaxed and happy, and when you feel like this you are better able to cope with stress and anxiety.

You can also help friends and others who may be feeling anxious or stressed. Listening to other people's problems and being there to give them a hug will help them and make you feel good about yourself. Have fun, relax and enjoy yourself.

ONE MORE WORD – POSITIVITY!

You might have heard a lot about positivity or being positive, but what does that mean exactly?

Through good and bad times

No one feels bright and happy and fully in control of their life all the time. Everyone has times when they feel sad, anxious or stressed — that's perfectly normal. The idea is to learn how to cope with the bad times, and being positive can help with this.

Being positive is remembering that nothing bad lasts forever. No matter how sad or angry or anxious you feel, it can and will get better. The bad feelings may pass naturally with time, or you can ask for advice from a professional person or a helpline to help you through, but either way you can and will feel better.

Positive thoughts

Positive thinking can help everyone every day. If you have a difficult task ahead, such as an exam or a class talk, instead of imagining the worst will happen, think the best will happen: you will do well in the exam and make a great presentation. If it's not perfect that doesn't matter. The fact that you tried your best is what is important.

TRY THIS!

Start the day saying something positive, such as: "Today will be a good day." It will get you in the right state of mind for the rest of the day. And smile! Even if you don't feel like it, it can make you feel better. Give it a try!

127

SOCIAL MEDIA AND YOU

YOUR EXPERIENCES ON SOCIAL
MEDIA HAVE A BIG EFFECT ON HOW
YOU THINK, FEEL AND BEHAVE, AND
HOW YOU BEHAVE ON SOCIAL MEDIA
CAN AFFECT OTHERS. THIS CHAPTER
HAS ADVICE ON HOW TO USE SOCIAL
MEDIA IN A FUN AND SAFE WAY SO
THAT YOU GET THE MOST OUT OF IT.

SOCIAL MEDIA — IT'S GREAT, RIGHT?

Social media can be brilliant for keeping in touch with friends and family, for doing homework research and finding out who's doing what where. But it's important to balance your online life with your offline life.

Life online

The time we spend online is linked to our physical and mental health, which affects how we think, feel and behave. We need to learn how to use social media in a fun and safe way and not let it become a habit that can take over and make us feel unhappy and anxious.

Be aware

Social media can cause all sorts of problems that happen before we know it. One of the worst of these is cyberbullying (see pages 154–156). In real life we can see how someone reacts to something we say or do, but online, we can't. When you can't see how someone is reacting to something you say, or how they are feeling, it might seem that it doesn't matter what you say. But by joining in with nasty comments that make fun of someone, you can make them feel scared, upset and hurt. And if you're the one being cyberbullied it can make your life a misery. We'll look at ways to beat cyberbullying later in this book.

Perfect people

We all love to see what everyone's wearing, where they are and who they're with. However, if we keep seeing super-filtered pictures of people looking fabulous, and having an amazing time, it might make us feel as if we're missing out. We could become jealous and unhappy with what we have. It can make us feel that we're not good enough just being who we are, and think we have to be like the 'perfect' people we see online.

To get the best out of social media you have to make sure that you stay in control, rather than let it control you. You can do this by remembering that most people only show the best bits of their life online and what you see online is not always how it really is at all.

132

SOCIAL MEDIA AND YOUR BRAIN

Scientists, doctors and psychologists are doing lots of research to find out how social media and the use of digital devices affect the way people – especially young people – think and feel.

Always online

Your brain is changing and growing rapidly all the time. It can be affected in all sorts of ways by too much screen time, which includes television, computers, tablets and mobile phones. Scientific studies have proved that spending too long on digital devices can be bad for mental and physical development in young people. It's tricky to say how much time is too much as it will vary from person to person. You just need to make sure that your offline life doesn't suffer because of the time you spend being online.

Positives and negatives

In 2018, the Safer Internet Centre did a survey of 2,000 8- to 17-year-olds, asking how social media affected them. Well over half said that chatting to friends online cheered them up and that in the past week they had seen something online that had made them feel inspired, excited and happy.

However, nearly half said that being online had made them feel sad, worried and anxious and that they had experienced mean comments or been excluded online. When social media goes well it can make you feel good and supported, but when it goes badly it can cause negative feelings and even lead to depression.

The effects of depression

Depression is a serious mental illness that can make people feel sad and hopeless. It makes someone lose interest in their friends, family, hobbies, themselves — everything. Depression causes lack of concentration and makes people find it really hard to do even simple everyday tasks.

How can social media cause depression?

People are using social media more and more to develop friendships, discover what we feel about ourselves and others and learn about the world around us. However, we are also judging ourselves by what happens online more than anything else.

We can start to obsess about online 'friends' and think we ourselves are only clever/pretty/cool if people online 'like' us and praise us. All this stress to compete can be exhausting, make people feel lonely and isolated, cause a negative self-image and lead to some people experiencing anxiety and depression.

OH, NO! FOMO!

Using social media to keep in touch with what's going on and what your friends are up to is great, but sometimes it can take over.

Fear of missing out

Social media helps to keep you in the loop about what is going on ... the latest funny video, shopping trip or chat about your favourite vlogger or sports club. Wanting to be part of what's going on is perfectly natural, but if you feel that you have to be online all the time so you don't miss out on any group chat, messaging, or invite, you could be experiencing FOMO — Fear of Missing Out.

136

Face-to-face v. online

- Think about why you feel you need to be online so much.
- Are you enjoying your time online?
- Are you missing out on face-to-face time with friends and family?
- Does being online make you feel happy or does it sometimes feel like something you have to do to keep your friends happy?
- Is it making you feel tired and anxious?

137

Keep it fun

When being online stops being fun, don't let it become a problem. It might be time to cut down on social media if:

- you spend more time with friends online than with friends in person
- you feel you need to be available online all the time to stay popular and keep your friends
- you think you might lose friends if you don't answer a message or text immediately.

These feelings can make you feel stressed and out of control, and this can lead to low self-esteem (how you value yourself). Take a deep breath, and take control of the situation. Here are some ideas to help you fight the FOMO:

• Plan how to cut back your hours online. Tell your friends that you are only going to be online at certain times of the day – say an hour in the afternoon and an hour in the evening, but not just before bedtime (see page 157).

• Instead of online chat, make a date to meet up in person. Visit friends at home, go for an ice-cream or take a picnic to the park.

TRY THIS!

Think about why you feel you might be missing out. Is it pressure being put on you by other people online, or pressure you are putting on yourself? Write down why you feel stressed about social media; sometimes writing down your worries and anxieties can make them seem less frightening and overwhelming.

EXCLUSION ZONE

Being deliberately left out of chats, games and messaging can be shocking and upsetting for the person who is being excluded.

Being ignored

It can be really hard if you are suddenly left out of chats and games, stop getting 'likes', are ignored online and not messaged by anyone. If this is happening to you, think about why it may have happened. Might your friends be reacting to something you've said online? It is so easy to respond quickly to a message or chat that sometimes the words come out wrong. And sometimes people can misread what someone has said and think they're being unkind, when they don't mean to be.

When we talk face-to-face we have people's facial expressions and body language to help us understand what is being said. Of course online we can't see people so we only have the words, and by themselves they can be misread. If you think this might have happened, ask a friend at school. If you have upset someone without realising it, explain it was a mistake. It is very brave to admit to your mistakes and good friends will understand if you did upset them by mistake.

Move on

Social media exclusion that happens over a long time is a form of cyberbullying that is intended to upset someone and make them feel bad about themselves. Being excluded online can make people feel alone, confused, sad and anxious. If this is happening to you, try switching off your social media for a while. The bullies will soon get bored. Set up new messaging groups with friends you trust or message people individually. Talk to your friends about what is happening and arrange to meet up in real life when they can give you all the latest news in person. If your friends don't seem to care, perhaps you need to think about making new friends who do care about how you feel.

Why me?

Don't think it's your fault if you are excluded.
People who exclude you online on purpose are not being
good friends. Keep positive, remember all your good
qualities and share your friendship with the friends that
are always there for you.

141

> I felt really terrible when I was suddenly
> ignored online. I thought I was a bad person.
> There had to be a reason why no one was
> talking to me. Then a friend told me someone
> had been spreading rumours about me that
> weren't true because they were jealous of me.
> That made me feel sad but it also made me
> feel better that it wasn't about me, but about
> how the other person felt. I stayed off instant
> messaging for a while anyway and I didn't
> really miss it.
>
> Sam, 14

PLEASE LIKE ME!

Studies have shown that more and more of us judge ourselves by the likes and comments we get from others on social media.

Liking being liked

Wanting to be liked is nothing new. Because humans are social creatures we all need to feel that we are liked and wanted by those people that matter to us – our family, friends and close schoolmates. But social media has taken being liked and accepted to a new level. Now we want everyone to 'like' us, even people we don't know.

The science bit

Experts have discovered that when we see someone has 'liked' us or when we get a positive comment online, this creates feelings of joy and happiness in the brain. These feelings only last for a short while, and they can become addictive. This means we need more and more likes and positive comments to feel happy.

Breaking the habit

If we rely on 'likes' to feel good about ourselves, and then stop getting them, or not enough of them, it can damage our self-esteem. We might begin to think we are worthless or not good enough, or stupid and ugly.

Step away

If this is happening to you, it may be you need to step away and take a break from social media and just stay in touch with close friends and family instead. Start thinking about yourself in a more positive way rather than relying on other people to boost your confidence.

Try a new hobby or join a group to get better at something you already enjoy, such as singing, painting, drama or sport. Being addicted to 'likes' is being recognised as a real problem so it is nothing to be ashamed of. But don't keep waiting for others to like you. Remember that you are more than good enough just the way you are.

144

TRY THIS!

If you feel you are losing confidence because you aren't getting enough 'likes' or good feedback on your postings, try some positive thinking. Take a few minutes every day to like yourself! When you're cleaning your teeth, getting dressed or walking to the bus stop, recite five great things about yourself. You might have lovely shiny hair, make the best sandwiches, help with the chores at home or be brilliant at football or art. Can't think of five things? Ask your family and close friends.

NOT REAL LIFE

It may seem obvious, but what happens on social media is not the same as in real life. People's lives in photos, blogs, tweets and videos can all be made to seem far more perfect than they are in reality.

145

Wanting more

Experts have found that when we see people online wearing the latest clothes, looking amazing and out with their mates doing fun things, it can have a negative impact on our mental health. It can make us feel dissatisfied with what we've got and keep us always wanting more. We get to a point where we will never be satisfied with what we have because someone online will always have something newer, more expensive or better. This can make us envious, unhappy and stressed.

Feeling lonely

Humans are social – we like to mix with other humans – but social media is almost the opposite of that. It's great at keeping us in touch with one another, but if people are glued to their digital devices, they're not interacting with others face-to-face. Spending too much time on social media can make us feel lonely even if we have loads of online friends. Also, seeing photos online of people having fun together or reading about what everyone else is doing, can sometimes make us feel isolated and alone.

Spot the signs

Do you:
• constantly compare yourself to your friends
• compare your achievements – how well or badly you've done – by what others have achieved
• think everyone else is having a better time than you
• lie awake at night worrying about how you can make your life more like those you see online?

146

Whatever you see online, remember that no one has a perfect life – everyone has both good and bad times. Most of us (even you, probably!) choose to put the best bits of our life on social media and ignore the boring, dull or unhappy bits. Don't be taken in; take control and make a plan to do more away from social media. Join a club or make a regular date to meet friends for a game or a chat. And don't forget about the people you live with! Can you check in with what they're doing and join in?

Take action

Rather than worry about what you haven't got or what you wish you had, focus on what you do have and how you can achieve what you want. If you have a burning ambition to be like someone online, whether it's a singer, a sports star or a scientist, make a plan about how you can achieve this. These professionals do a lot of hard work, even if they make it look easy online.

BODY IMAGE

Body image is what people think of their bodies and how they see themselves when they look in the mirror.

All change

As you grow, your body will change, especially when you start to go through puberty. You might become aware of getting more hair on your body or your body shape changing. You might begin to compare how you look with your friends and with people you admire on social media. If someone feels that they don't look as good as people online, this can begin to affect their self-esteem and their body image. They might think they are too tall, too short, too fat or too thin, for example.

Tricks of the trade

Bloggers and celebrities spend hours putting on make-up, getting the lighting right or preparing a single shot to look absolutely perfect. They use filters and photo-editing apps and can take hundreds of photos before getting the one that is just right. In real life they probably don't look anything like as cool as they do online. There is no perfect body shape or perfect way to look. We are all different and we should be proud of that.

Care, but be aware

It's perfectly natural to care about how you look, but
if you find yourself obsessing about your appearance
and feel unhappy about it all the time, you could have
a negative body image. People who feel really unhappy
about how they look may be more likely to suffer from
eating disorders such as bulimia, anorexia or binge eating.
If you feel this is happening to you, talk to a trusted adult,
maybe a family member, a friend's parent or a teacher at
school. Or ask your parents or carers to take you to see
a doctor.

No one is going to think any the worse of you because you asked for help. In fact you are being very grown up facing the problem and trying to do something about it.

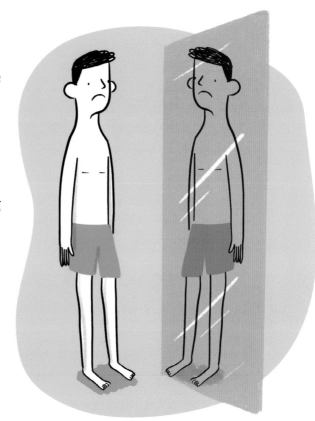

Online everyone looks so pretty with smooth skin. My skin was blotchy and I had freckles. Mum caught me putting on her foundation and asked why I needed it. I told her to cover up my freckles because they made me look ugly. She found a picture of one of my favourite singers without any make-up – and she had freckles! Now I see lots of models with freckles and it makes me feel better.

Anna, 11

DEVELOPING SELF-WORTH

Comparing yourself to other people is never going to make you feel good. You have to learn to love who you are and develop self-worth.

It's worth the work

Self-worth is how much you value and respect yourself — your body, your skills, your personality, everything about you.

Self-worth is being able to like who you are no matter what anyone else says about you. It's about being proud of who you are.

A good body image is an important part of having a strong sense of self-worth. Some people may need to work harder than others to accept their body image, but it's well worth it. Do things you enjoy and that make you feel good about yourself and your life.

If you're following someone online who makes you feel miserable about how you look, unfollow them. Find another blog that focuses on skills and ideas rather than appearance. For example, look for sites that can help you improve your sporting skills or can teach you a new craft that you'll really enjoy.

Only human

Self-worth is not all about how you look. It's about realising that everyone is different and we all have lots of good points and a few not so good points – that's called being human! Good self-worth means feeling positive about yourself and your life. Spending too much time online comparing yourself to others is unlikely to help you develop your sense of self-worth.

Achieve great things

Find blogs written by people who have achieved something special. This will give you inspiration and help spark creative ideas about how you can do great things. Go online to find out about interesting things happening in your area that might be something new for you to learn about or get involved with. Or find out about places to visit locally that you can go to with your family.

TRY THIS!

Think about new things to do offline and online. Plan a video call with a friend or family member you haven't seen for a long time. Organise a trip to the park for a game or a picnic with your best friend, family or a group of friends. Spending time with people we love and care about and that make us happy is one of the best ways to boost self-worth and keep us feeling positive.

CYBERBULLYING

Being bullied on a phone, website, app or game is cyberbullying and can have a serious effect on mental health.

Hiding behind anonymity

On games, messaging sites, social media sites and in chat rooms it is very easy to humiliate and threaten people, tell lies about people, start rumours and post embarrassing photos. Many people who wouldn't bully face-to-face feel safe bullying online as they can remain anonymous.

Cyberbullying can happen at any time of day or night –
if it is happening to you it can feel like there is nowhere
to hide. If you stick to friending just people you know
personally and trust, there is less chance that you will
be cyberbullied.

Block the bullies

Cyberbullying can make people withdrawn, anxious and
depressed. It can affect their home life, schoolwork and
friendships. In some cases it can lead to self-harming
and suicide. If you are being cyberbullied on social media
speak to a trusted adult about what is happening. Block
or delete the person who is bullying you. If you're not sure
what might be abuse, and whether you should report it to

155

the police, look at
pages 172–174 for
organisations
you can contact
for help.

It's serious

Everyone takes
cyberbullying
very seriously,
including
teachers. If one
teacher can't
help you, speak to
someone else at
school who can.

The school has a duty to make sure that there is nothing in your personal life that is damaging your ability to do your schoolwork or to be safe, happy and healthy. If you would prefer to talk safely to someone you don't know via a helpline, there are contact details on pages 172-174.

Stop and think

Think before you post on social media. It's easy to post a comment about a photo that you think is funny but it could upset the person whose photo it is. And it could result in other followers turning on you!

"

When I was being cyberbullied on social media my friends told me to ignore it but I couldn't think about anything else. Eventually I started just messaging my mates until everything calmed down. My mates were great about it... they would message me to let me know about changes to plans and where to meet. The bullying has stopped now, and I didn't miss being on social media as much as I thought I would.

Ravi, 14

"

SLEEP WELL

Social media platforms never switch off, but you need to. Sleep is important for everyone for good physical and mental health.

sleep – it's good for you

Research shows that preteens need between 9 to 12 hours' sleep a night. Lack of sleep affects you physically and mentally. It can cause mood swings, make you feel anxious and grumpy, and unable to concentrate on schoolwork, and can lead to depression.

Not getting enough sleep means you don't really enjoy yourself when you're with your friends, either, because you may feel sleepy or be irritable with everyone or your brain may feel groggy.

Sweet dreams

During sleep your body repairs cells and releases growth hormones. It strengthens your immune system that keeps you physically healthy and your nervous system that keeps you feeling good. When we sleep we all dream (though sometimes we don't remember them when we wake up). Dreams are really important to our mental and physical health.

158

When we dream, our brain is helping us to sort through problems we had during the day and to come up with solutions. In this way, dreams can help us to deal with something that may have upset us during the day. Dreams can also help to turn our experiences into memories.

Switch off

Experiments have proved that the blue light from digital screens can affect our sleep cycles. It can also affect the quality of our sleep so that we feel groggy in the morning — not good if you've got a test or maths lesson first thing or an important sports game. You should switch off at least an hour before you go to sleep to let your brain adjust and make sure you get a really good night's sleep.

159

If you find you wake up and check your phone or tablet in the night, you need to take control of the situation and set yourself a nightly routine. Check all your messages an hour before bed and then leave the device downstairs or ask an adult in your household to keep it with them until morning.

ONLINE HELP

One of the best places to go for help if you're having trouble on social media, is ... online! There are charities and specialist websites that offer advice and support.

Support and understanding

Many charities have websites that help and support young people having a tough time at home, school or online. We've listed some on pages 172–174 and there might be others local to your area, too. Do an online search for a site specifically aimed at kids. Being scared and sad can make you feel very alone. It can make you feel as if you're the only person suffering or being threatened.

Online you can find advice and support and read about how others who are the same age as you have coped with similar experiences.

Never agree to meet up with anyone from online, and if someone suggests you meet, tell an adult.

Some charities also have counsellors you can talk to. They are specially trained to listen to you and give you support and advice. They will never be shocked or angry at what you say, so you do not need to feel guilty, embarrassed or ashamed when talking to them. You can be honest and open.

Chats and phone calls

If you are worried about your thoughts, feelings or behaviour, joining an online group can be a great help in expressing how you feel, sharing your fears and worries and realising that you are not the only person going through a tough time. But you still need to be aware of online safety whilst finding help online. Don't ever post your name or any personal details, not even which school you go to. They are specially trained to listen to you and givThey

> " *When I went through a time when I was feeling really bad about myself, I rang a charity helpline. The lady I talked to was really understanding and helpful. It made me feel better to talk it through and know I wasn't the only one feeling this way.*
>
> **Ned, 13**
> "

Offline works, too!

Sometimes people can feel that their negative thoughts and sad feelings are getting too much for them. If you ever feel like that, talking to someone you trust may help, but try to do this face-to-face if you can. Putting very personal stuff online about your deepest feelings and fears could lead to other people making nasty comments or trying to take advantage of how bad you feel. And talking in person is so much better anyway – you can't have a hug on the phone!

TAKE A TECH BREAK

Spending too much time online or just fancy a change? Why not give yourself and your friends a tech break challenge?

Start something new

Being on social media all the time might stop you trying out new things, such as an after-class sports club, or make you feel cross and anxious when the family suggest a weekend camping, for example, where there are no digital signals. If the idea of no tech makes you feel really stressed, a tech break could be exactly what you need.

How much is too much?

It is difficult to say how much time spent online is too much as it depends on the individual person, how they use social media and how social media affects them. Here are some signs to look out for:

- Do you believe you can't cope without social media?
- Do you feel anxious and panicky when you're not online?
- Do you stay awake at night so you can check messages and social sites during the night?
- Is your schoolwork suffering because of your social media life?
- Do you lie about how much time you spend online?
- Would you rather be online than with family and friends?

If you feel worried about how you're handling social media, talk to an adult you trust about how you are feeling. They can help you manage how you spend your time online. Don't think that what you're feeling is silly or trivial or not worth worrying anyone about. Social media is a powerful force and sometimes we all need help in how to handle it.

Face-to-face

You can end up spending so much time on your favourite sites that you may forget to actually meet people face-to-face! Once you start spending time with your friends, you'll soon realise how much more enjoyable it is to talk and properly experience being together, instead of everyone being glued to their phones all the time.

> ## TRY THIS!
> *Set yourself a tech break challenge.*
> *Try and stick to only an hour a day on social media. Or switch it off completely for a whole weekend or a week. It might seem a bit strange at first, but think about all the other things you can do instead!*

ONE MORE WORD - SELFIES!

We all do it - with our best friends, family and pets. Selfies can be great, but you need to be careful about which people you share them with.

special moments

Posting pictures of yourself online to share special moments with your friends and family is a great way to keep in touch and create memories for years to come. However, be careful when you post selfies.

Showing your best friend or granny your latest holiday photos of you on the beach in your swimming gear or wearing your favourite pyjamas is fine, but make sure you don't send personal photos to everyone you're linked to online. Be aware that people you don't know that well may make comments that could make you feel bad — and no one needs that!

Share with care

When you post pictures of yourself online you have no control of where they end up or who can get hold of them. What seems funny and cute to share with your friends now might be embarrassing when you're older. Think about what you're posting online ... if you wouldn't want your parents, teachers, carers or the whole school to see it, don't post it! When you do share selfies, make sure it's just with your close friends and family, not with people you don't know that well.

GLOSSARY

ADOLESCENCE the period following puberty, when a young person develops into an adult

AMYGDALA a part of the brain that affects your emotions, such as fear

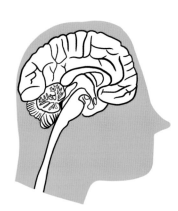

ANOREXIA an emotional illness where someone stops eating because they believe they are overweight

BRAIN STEM the part of your brain connected to your spine

ANXIOUS feeling worried, nervous or uneasy about how something is going to turn out

BULIMIA an emotional illness where a person eats too much and then makes themselves sick or stops eating

ARTHRITIS a painful disease of the joints

CEREBELLUM the part of the brain that makes your muscles work

168

BINGING doing something to excess

CEREBRUM the part of your brain that controls your muscles, such as your heart and lungs

BODY IMAGE your idea of how you see your body and how you think it should look

CIRCADIAN RHYTHM your natural body clock

COMPULSIVE EATING eating lots of food in an uncontrolled way

CONFIDENCE belief in yourself and your ability to do things

CONFUSED not thinking clearly

CYBERBULLYING being called names or threatened online or being deliberately excluded from online activities by other people

DEHYDRATED dry and thirsty, needing water

DEPRESSION an illness that affects us physically (not able to sleep, always feeling tired, no energy) and mentally (feeling anxious, tearful, hopeless and alone). There are many different symptoms.

EATING DISORDERS a mental illness in which people eat far too little or far too much food and are unhappy with their bodies

EMOTIONS feelings, such as sadness, happiness, fear and anger

EMOTIONAL AWARENESS being aware of your feelings, why you feel that way and what makes you feel that way

EMOTIONAL HEALTH how you feel mentally, about yourself and the world around you

EMOTIONAL INTELLIGENCE to be able to recognise your emotions, why you feel them and to cope with them

EMPATHY being able to understand and share other people's feelings

ENDORPHINS hormones released into the brain and body that make you feel good

ENERGISED feeling full of energy

FATAL deadly

GROWTH HORMONES substances released into your body that help the body to grow and develop

169

GROWTH SPURTS when bones and muscles grow quickly during puberty

HORMONES chemical substances released into your body that affect how you grow and how you feel

HUMILIATE make a person feel stupid and embarrassed in front of other people

HYDRATED having plenty of water

IMMUNE SYSTEM the part of the body that protects us from diseases

IRRATIONAL not able to be explained

MINDFULNESS being aware of your thoughts and feelings moment by moment

MOOD SWINGS quick changes in mood, such as feeling happy one minute and sad the next

NERVOUS SYSTEM the part of your body that controls everything you do. It is made up of your brain, spinal cord and nerves

NEURONS also known as nerve cells, these carry electrical messages around the body via the nervous system

NUTRIENTS parts of food that we need to stay healthy

OBSESSIVE COMPULSIVE DISORDER (OCD) a mental health condition in which a person has frequent, unwanted thoughts or feelings that make them feel that they have to repeat particular actions

OVERTHINKING thinking and analysing something too much in a way that is harmful

OVERWHELMING feeling that something like a situation or emotion is too big or difficult to handle

PANIC ATTACK a sudden and overwhelming feeling of fear that can cause a pounding heart, sweating and shaking

PITUITARY GLAND a part of the brain that controls several of the body's functions, such as growth

POSITIVE good, confident, able to cope

POSITIVITY being positive and thinking things will get better and work out well

PUBERTY the time when you develop from a child into an adult

REASONING thinking about something in a sensible and logical way

RITUALS a series of actions that have a special meaning

SELF-ESTEEM the way you feel about yourself and your belief in what you can achieve

SIBLINGS brothers and sisters

SLUGGISH feeling slow and tired

STRESS emotional and mental strain when it feels as if everything is getting too much

TOXINS a type of poison

TRAUMA a very distressing experience

UNIQUE the only one in the world

VISUALISE see something in your head

WORTHLESSNESS having no use or value

171

FURTHER INFORMATION

Websites and helplines

If you feel overwhelmed by any of the issues you've read about in this book, or need advice, check out a website or call a helpline and talk to someone who will understand.

www.brainline.org/content/2009/05/who-me-self-esteem-for-people-with-disabilities.html
How to boost self-esteem regardless of disabilities.

www.bbc.co.uk/bitesize/articles/zwnw8hv
A collection of tips, advice and stories to support your mental health.

www.childline.org.uk/info-advice/your-feelings/mental-health
Find out about mental health issues, meet others, message or call the 24-hour helpline for advice or someone who'll just listen.
Telephone: 0800 1111

www.kidshealth.org/en/kids/feeling
Check out what causes good and bad feelings and how to manage your emotions.

www.kooth.com
Free online support from professionals, real-life experiences, a place to talk and write about your worries with people who understand.

netaddiction.com/childrenonline
Aimed at parents and carers, this explains online addiction, signs of online addiction, how to prevent it and how to get help.

www.samaritans.org
A place where anyone can go for advice and comfort. The helpline number is 116 123.

173

www.supportline.org.uk
A charity giving emotional support to children and young people. The helpline number is 01708 765200.

www.themix.org.uk
Free helpline, email or join their webchat.
Freephone: 0808 808 4994
(13:00–23:00 daily).

www.youngminds.org.uk
Information and advice for children and young people experiencing bullying, stress and mental or emotional anxieties.

New Zealand and Australia

www.healthdirect.gov.au/partners/kids-helpline
A helpline for young people that gives advice, counselling and support. The number is 1800 55 1800.

www.sane.org/get-help
Online and phone help for mental and emotional issues with a dedicated helpline for young people. The helpline number is 1800 18 7263.

www.lifeline.org.nz/services/kidsline
Helpline run by specially trained young volunteers to help kids and teens deal with troubling issues and problems. The number is 0800 543 354.

Note to parents and teachers

Every effort has been made by the Publishers to ensure that these websites are suitable for children, that they are of the highest educational value, and that they contain no inappropriate or offensive material. However, because of the nature of the Internet, it is impossible to guarantee that the contents of these sites will not be altered. We strongly advise that Internet access is supervised by a responsible adult.

Books

Grab a book and find somewhere quiet to read about things that might be concerning you or just to be inspired.

12 Hacks to Happiness
by Honor Head, Franklin Watts, 2020

Keep Your Cool. How to Deal with Life's Worries and Stress.
by Dr Aaron Balick, Franklin Watts, 2020

Dealing with Bullying
by Jane Lacey, Franklin Watts, 2019

The Unworry Book
by Alice James, Usborne, 2019

You Are Awesome: Find your confidence and dare to be brilliant at (almost) anything
by Matthew Syed, Wren and Rook, 2018

Dr Christian's Guide to Growing Up Online
by Dr Christian Jessen, Scholastic, 2018

Create Your Own Happy
by Penny Alexander and Becky Goddard-Hill, Collins, 2018

Hello Happy! Mindful Kids: An activity book for young people who sometimes feel sad or angry
by Stephanie Clarkson, Dr Sharie Coombes and Katie Abey, Studio Press, 2017

Dr Christian's Guide to You
by Dr Christian Jessen, Scholastic, 2016

The Kids' Guide to Staying Awesome and in Control
by Lauren Brukner, Jessica Kingsley Publishers, 2014

Texts, Tweets, Trolls and Teens
by Anita Naik, Wayland 2014

Bullies, Cyberbullies and Frenemies
by Michele Elliot, Wayland, 2013

Self Esteem and Being You
by Anita Naik, Wayland, 2013

INDEX